PHILIP HE

POWDER HER FACE

AN OPERA IN TWO ACTS
AND EIGHT SCENES

SET TO MUSIC BY
THOMAS ADÈS

FABER *ff* MUSIC

First published in 1995 by Faber Music Ltd
3 Queen Square London WC1N 3AU
Cover illustration: *Old Man on a Swing, Among Demons* by Goya
Printed in England by Halstan & Co Ltd

ISBN 0 571 51611 4

Powder Her Face was commissioned by Almeida Opera
and first performed by Valdine Anderson, Roger Bryson,
Jill Gomez and Niall Morris with the Almeida Opera, conducted by
Brad Cohen and directed by David Farr, in the Everyman Theatre,
Cheltenham on 1 July 1995, as part of the 1995 Cheltenham Festival.
Further performances took place at the Almeida Theatre, London
on 5, 9, 14, 17 and 22 July 1995

For Thomas Blaikie

CAST

Duchess
Hotel Manager
Electrician
Maid

POWDER HER FACE

(LAUGHTER-PROLOGUE)

ONE
Nineteen Ninety

(As lights rise Electrician as Duchess in a very camp Statue of Liberty pose – immense fur coat and high heels. Apparently alone on the stage – actually behind him on a bed in the darkness is Maid, laughing (taking over from the orchestra's laughing). When her laughter subsides the scene begins.)

MAID: What happened then, your Grace?

ELECTRICIAN AS DUCHESS:
> I was betrayed, girl. My life is one long sorrow.
> There are moments in my life.
> There are moments in my life as of no other life.
> Moments of anguish *(melodramatically)* and betrayal.

MAID: But why your Grace did this happen to you? Why to you?

(Lights begin to rise and Maid is revealed sitting on a bed – so big she seems a small child, bouncing up and down – in a fabulously hideous gilt and pastel hotel room. At the back a pair of double doors. To the right is a huge chest, open and overflowing with clothes. A dressing table with detritus, wig stand, jewel boxes. A stuffed Pekinese lying on the floor. An old-fashioned gramophone.)

ELECTRICIAN AS DUCHESS:
> I cannot say.
> I was beautiful. I was famous. I was young.
> I was rich, girl.
> What more do they need? Do they need purity to crow over?
> They had it. Do they need innocence?
> I was innocent, girl.
>   *(sudden vulgarity, drops arms)*
> Girl, I had innocence.

*(Maid laughs immoderately – shrill, horrible laugh –
and Electrician as Duchess back to Statue of Liberty
abruptly.)*
I had my life, and it was good.
I was beautiful, and it was good.
Let me tell you about me. Let me tell you about my
life as a famous beauty.
They wrote operas about me.
(laugh)
They wrote novels about me.
(laugh. Song starts in the orchestra about now)
They painted portraits of me that won every prize in
London.
(grand gesture to spotlit blank wall)
They wrote songs about me.
You know that song. Everyone knows that song –
Love me
Why don't you suck me off until you can't take
more
I'll really ram it in your jaw*
Because you practise every night fellatio
It's the most delightful art you know. . .

*(*Enter Duchess, behind. Tiny, terrifying, dressed in another fur coat, even more
grotesquely enormous. Maid still laughing and laughing. Electrician drops out of
pose, pulls wig off.)*

DUCHESS:	I see. This is what it has come to. Take off my coat. *(He takes off the coat he is wearing)* Who are you, boy?
ELECTRICIAN:	Your grace, I came to mend your teasmade.
DUCHESS:	My – teasmade. Have you mended it?
ELECTRICIAN:	Your grace, I couldn't mend it.
DUCHESS:	Why cannot you mend it?
ELECTRICIAN:	Your grace. It's just too old. They stopped making teasmades like this, you know; you want to buy a new one.
MAID:	I brought you tea, madam. *(Indicates a tray)*

6

DUCHESS:	It is too old.
	Very well. *(Waits for the maid to pour it – she still bouncing on the bed.)* Where is the tea, girl –
MAID:	I brought you the tea, madam. It's there, can't you see.
DUCHESS:	Who are you, anyway? Why aren't you the usual girl?
MAID:	I'm just filling in, madam. Just for the afternoon.
DUCHESS:	I like to have my usual maid.
MAID:	It can't be helped.

(Duchess gives in and goes to pour the tea.)

DUCHESS:	There is no milk –
MAID:	It's on the tray.
DUCHESS:	It isn't there –
MAID:	It's in the pots.

(They face each other.)

DUCHESS:	How you speak to me.
MAID:	Are you checking out today, madam.

(Electrician stifles guilty gasp/laugh.)

(Pantomime: Duchess picks up a small plastic pot of milk and examines it. She tries to open it but succeeds only in splattering it over her fur. Maid goes off into a fresh fit of laughter.)

MAID: You know the men who make the pots for milk
They say they've got more money than the Queen.

DUCHESS: *(Imperious)*
I knew that would happen, horrid thing;
It must be cleaned; it stinks, it stinks, I always know
When things will stink. Take it from me, bring me
My other fur, bring me shoes, show me tea gowns
That I shall choose among.
Take it from me, the stinking thing.
Bring me pearls before six and diamonds after,

                         Bring me scent, tiny scents; fetch these things
                         And fetch my life.

MAID: *(takes coat from her)*
                         Yes Madam. Yes Madam. Glorious fur and glorious
                         smell
                         The perfume of it, the expense, the money –

ELECTRICIAN: What's it called –

MAID: Her perfume –

ELECTRICIAN: Her perfume –

MAID: Joy. It's called Joy.

DUCHESS: And here I am, and my glorious smell,
                         My scent, which I have worn forever, which
                         outlasts fashion
                         And outlasts time, and lasts forever
                         Like nothing, like nothing else;
                         And am I good? Am I heaven? When they come for
                         me,
                         When they see me, won't they be silenced, won't
                         they be struck dumb and long to be folded
                         To the expense and money of my cladded breast?

ELECTRICIAN and MAID:
                         Joy.

MAID: The expense, the money.

ELECTRICIAN and MAID:
                         The buying of Joy.
                         And in the end it evaporates into air –
                         Like everything. The stuff, the money,
                         It goes, all goes –

ELECTRICIAN: And hers has gone for good.

MAID: Gone for good.

ELECTRICIAN: You can't have everything –

MAID: Not everything –

ELECTRICIAN: Not forever –

ELECTRICIAN and MAID:	
	Never –
	Nothing –

MAID:	Gone,

ELECTRICIAN:	Taken,

MAID:	Seized.

ELECTRICIAN:	He's on his way.

DUCHESS: Everything will be the same forever now;
Will last forever; from now there is no future.
From now there is nothing; there was a future once
because there was a past;
But the doors will be opened, and the taxis draw up,
And nothing walk in, and nothing step out,
Because there is nothing left, except me –

ELECTRICIAN and MAID:
Here he comes.

DUCHESS: And the Duke, my Duke, my better angel;
And here he comes. Here he comes.

(At the back of the stage a door opens – very brilliantly lit from behind – and the shape of a man can be seen. The door shuts slowly during the Interlude.)

TWO
Nineteen Thirty Four

(Same room but now the drawing room of a country house. Maid is now Maid as Confidante. Electrician is now Electrician as Lounge Lizard. During the interlude they have been dressing from the Trunk, a sort of child's dressing-up box. Maid in feather boa and pearls and cloche hat, Electrician in white suit and absurd thirties white hat, jacket without shirt. Duchess still at stage front, unlit.)

MAID AS CONFIDANTE:
Of course she's done well.

ELECTRICIAN AS LOUNGE LIZARD:
He treated her pretty badly, that beast. Mr Freeling.
She deserves everything she got out of the divorce.
He treated her like a brute –

MAID AS CONFIDANTE:
>She treated him like a banker –

ELECTRICIAN AS LOUNGE LIZARD:
>He beat her –

MAID AS CONFIDANTE:
>She beat him, in the end –

ELECTRICIAN AS LOUNGE LIZARD:
>Still, one looks at him, and one knows he could beat his wife.
>And as for her, she has the look of one who will let herself be beaten for money.
>But Mr Freeling. *(confidentially)* I shouldn't trust him.

MAID AS CONFIDANTE:
>You dine with him once a week.

ELECTRICIAN AS LOUNGE LIZARD:
>We all do, darling, but I shouldn't trust him.
>She deserves better than him.

MAID AS CONFIDANTE:
>She deserves nothing.
>She'll get better than him. *(laughter)*
>Watch her practise on the Duke, when he arrives.

ELECTRICIAN AS LOUNGE LIZARD:
>It's more than practising.
>She'll catch him. She's got the knack.

DUCHESS: *(stage front, as if looking out of a window)*
>Here he comes. I know it. I know it.

ELECTRICIAN AS LOUNGE LIZARD:
>He won't be here yet, darling.

MAID AS CONFIDANTE:
>He'll be here quite soon enough. And we'll be bored of him before he's gone.

ELECTRICIAN AS LOUNGE LIZARD:
>Not me.

DUCHESS:
>Nor me.

ELECTRICIAN AS LOUNGE LIZARD:
He's heaven.

DUCHESS: Perfect heaven.

ELECTRICIAN AS LOUNGE LIZARD:
And charming.

DUCHESS: So charming.

MAID AS CONFIDANTE:
And rich.

DUCHESS: So rich.

ELECTRICIAN AS LOUNGE LIZARD:
The richest –

MAID AS CONFIDANTE, DUCHESS and ELECTRICIAN AS LOUNGE LIZARD:
Richard!!!
(They all laugh: exaggeratedly polite)

(What follows is an aria for the Duchess and a simultaneous duet between Electrician as Lounge Lizard and Maid as Confidante. Not a terzetto.)

DUCHESS: I could never grow bored of dukedoms. But now I'm so bored.
It's an hour before the Duke comes. There's an hour before tea.
Two hours before dressing. Three before cocktails.
Four before dinner. And an age before bed.
These hours to fill, hours upon hours with nothing but chatter.
And at the end of it, there's sleep.

MAID AS CONFIDANTE:
Did you hear about Poppy?

ELECTRICIAN AS LOUNGE LIZARD:
Poppy?

MAID AS CONFIDANTE:
Poppy. She was five months gone when she went to the Duke, and he wouldn't do a thing.

DUCHESS: *(trying to break in)*
But the Duke, you say –

MAID AS CONFIDANTE:
You know how she was before all this, but you
simply wouldn't believe.
She was a wreck, a perfect wreck.

DUCHESS: *(to herself)*
I hear he's so handsome. I hear he's so rich.

ELECTRICIAN AS LOUNGE LIZARD:
He said it wasn't his. *On chuchote.*

MAID AS CONFIDANTE:
It was his. He's a duke, but he's no gentleman.

DUCHESS: *(to herself)*
I hear he's good to tenants. I hear he's a demon in
the sack.

MAID AS CONFIDANTE:
And now she's dead, and I told him, and he laughed.

ELECTRICIAN AS LOUNGE LIZARD:
He laughed.

MAID AS CONFIDANTE and ELECTRICIAN AS LOUNGE LIZARD:
He laughed and now she's dead.

DUCHESS: I hear he gives to charity.
I hear him coming. . .

MAID AS CONFIDANTE and ELECTRICIAN AS LOUNGE LIZARD:
She's dead. But it makes no odds. *(gesture to Duchess)*
She'll marry him soon enough.

ELECTRICIAN: She deserves him.

MAID: You're right.

DUCHESS: I hear him coming.

MAID AS CONFIDANTE and ELECTRICIAN AS LOUNGE LIZARD:
And they'll kill each other.

DUCHESS: I hear him coming.

MAID AS CONFIDANTE:
No darling, it was just the man.

(PANTOMIME. Duchess sits down patting a cushion beside her. Electrician as Lounge Lizard moves to join her. Duchess indicates she meant Maid. Electrician as Lounge Lizard wanders away, faintly rebuffed. Maid goes to sit by Duchess.)

ELECTRICIAN AS LOUNGE LIZARD: *(Distractedly, picks up a magazine)*
　　　　　　Respectability stretch.

(Puts it down – goes over to the gramophone on the floor and starts the record that is on it.)

　　　　　　Forget restrictions
　　　　　　Legality
　　　　　　No more commandments
　　　　　　When your eyes are fixed on me.
　　　　　　There's nothing in all the world
　　　　　　Like being curled around your little finger
　　　　　　Divinest feeling
　　　　　　Dizzying touch
　　　　　　But for Mr Freeling
　　　　　　I would float right through the ceiling
　　　　　　And admit my heart is reeling
　　　　　　With this electric feeling
　　　　　　That I love you
　　　　　　Why don't you love me back until we're ninety five
　　　　　　Your love is keeping me alive
　　　　　　And I've succumbed to your unchecked ability
　　　　　　Chased away respectability
　　　　　　Stretch me out
　　　　　　Touch the feelings that we feel when we collide
　　　　　　You're my ideal
　　　　　　So see you tonight.

DUCHESS:　　Divinest feeling. They wrote that song for me, you know. They wrote so many songs for me. Dizzying touch.

MAID AS CONFIDANTE:
　　　　　　I know.

DUCHESS:　　Sometimes I wonder –

MAID AS CONFIDANTE:
　　　　　　What do you wonder, darling?

DUCHESS: Sometimes I wonder whether anyone will ever write songs for me, or love me ever again.

MAID AS CONFIDANTE:
Of course they will, darling.

DUCHESS: Yes, I suppose they will. The Duke would do.

MAID AS CONFIDANTE:
To write songs, darling?

DUCHESS: To buy them, darling.

ELECTRICIAN AS LOUNGE LIZARD:
Who said it mattered?
What the public prints will say
They should be flattered
Now one reads them every day.
They say our love is queer and sinful and blind
But darling don't let panic muddle your mind
For if you ran away
Every night and every day
I would pursue you
I'd walk a thousand miles
Endure your guiles
For just one chance that you'd hold me
Touch me
Love me
I'm in your clutches
Duchess
Mine.

DUCHESS: Divinest feeling.

MAID AS CONFIDANTE:
Darling, I think that's him.

DUCHESS: That's him?

(She leaps off the bed, takes the needle forcefully off the record player and runs to the window, i.e. the front of the stage.)

That's his car. He's in the house.
It can't be long. I'll see him soon.

(Door at back of stage opens, and in the same way as the last scene, a man's figure is outlined against brilliant backlighting. Maid as Confidante and Electrician as Lounge Lizard stand up.)

(She turns round, suddenly seeing him. Abrupt silence.)

HOTEL MANAGER AS DUKE:
Dear Mrs Freeling.

DUCHESS: Dear Duke.

(The door behind him slams violently. Cue for black-out and Interlude.)

(During the Interlude, Duchess and Duke stand apart facing front, two imposing figures, half-lit. Electrician and Maid dress Duke and Duchess in wedding clothes.)

THREE
Nineteen Thirty Six

Hotel Manager as Duke stays where he is through interlude – an impressive half-lit figure at the back of the stage. As the interlude comes to an end the lights go down to complete black, where the scene begins.

The following pantomime is seen not through being lit, but as if through flash-bulbs being let off every now and again from the flies. The stage is otherwise at first utterly dark. Thirteen tableaux, happening at intervals throught the following Fancy Aria.

1. *Hotel Manager as Duke and Duchess before Electrician as Priest.*
2. *Hotel Manager as Duke and Duchess embracing. Electrician as Priest sitting on the ground.*
3. *Duchess sandwiched between Electrician as Priest and Hotel Manager as Duke.*
4. *Electrician as Priest and Duchess kissing. Hotal Manager as Duke watches.*
5. *Hotel Manager as Duke and Duchess before Electrician as Priest.*
6. *Hotel Manager as Duke and Duchess before Electrician as Priest.*
7. *Electrician as Priest and Duchess embracing. Hotel Manager as Duke sitting on the ground.*

8. *Dispatched to different parts of the stage – as if caught in conversation with invisible guests.*
9. *Standing in a line – Duchess (central)veiled.*
10. *Lying in a pile on top of each other.*
11. *Standing in a line – Electrician as Priest veiled.*
12. *Standing in a line – Hotel Manager as Duke veiled.*
13. *Electrician as Priest and Hotel Manager as Duke and Duchess collapsed in a heap on top of each other on the bed. They stay there writhing lewdly during the Interlude (until curtain).*

MAID AS WAITRESS:
>Fancy.
>Fancy being rich.
>Fancy being lovely.
>Fancy having money to waste, and not minding it.
>They've got too much money, and nothing to do.
>Nothing to do, but come to a wedding in the middle of the week. *(laughter)*
>Only fancy.
>Fancy eating lobster in the middle of the week standing up.
>Fancy drinking champagne in the middle of the day and too drunk to worry and twelve and six a bottle.
>Fancy being her.
>The food's so lovely, though.
>Shining like water, all under aspic.
>Cut fruit in aspic, vegetable shapes, whole chicken.
>Fish swimming in aspic, caught in stiff water.
>Preserved.
>She doesn't look happy. She looks rich. *(laughter)*
>I wouldn't want to be happy if I was as rich as that.
>I'd be like her. I'd marry rich men.
>I wouldn't live in two rooms in Kentish Town, I'll tell you that for nothing.
>I'd wear a tiara for breakfast.
>I'd sleep in an hotel if I felt like it in the afternoon.
>I'd eat nothing that wasn't lovely in aspic and hard work for someone.

I'd buy a whole shop full of diamonds and have it
delivered in a carriage if I felt like it.
And I would feel like it, and I'd look as miserable as
sin.
Just like her.
Just fancy being her.

(She takes a bottle of champagne, and, over the next four lines, pulls the cork out.)

Fancy putting milk and almonds in your bath.
Fancy your underclothes costing thirty shillings the
ounce.
Yes, fancy having nothing to do but wait for the
man for your hair and the girl for your skin and the
boy with the telegram with reply paid for.
Fancy purchasing a Duke.

(The bottle explodes. She pours it into a glass while singing, and carries on pouring into the overflowing glass until the bottle is quite empty and the table sopping wet.)

That's what I want.
That's what you want.
You'd love it.

(She takes the glass of champagne over to the bed and hands it to the Electrician as Priest, who drinks it in one go – with his mouth shut, so that all the champagne runs down his face and down his clothes. The Maid as Waitress walks away. He throws the glass after her, and seizes the Duchess and kisses her violently. She acquiesces.)

FOUR
Nineteen Fifty Three

(Duchess alone on the bed with a telephone. White dressing gown, head wrapped in a white towel. Possibly with a face mask on. She dials. Hotel Manager as Laundryman answers.)

HOTEL MANAGER AS LAUNDRYMAN:
How may I help you?

DUCHESS: Room service?

HOTEL MANAGER AS LAUNDRYMAN:
              This is the laundry, ma'am.

DUCHESS: *(putting the telephone down)*
              I wanted room service.

(Dials again, more deliberately. Hotel Manager as Other Guest answers.)

HOTEL MANAGER AS OTHER GUEST:
              Cindy? Is that you, Cindy, honey?

DUCHESS: No, this is – I wanted room service.

HOTEL MANAGER AS OTHER GUEST:
              Me too, sweetheart.

(Orchestra laughs as Duchess puts telephone down. Picks up phone and dials again with exaggerated deliberation.)

ELECTRICIAN AS WAITER:
              Room –

ELECTRICIAN AS WAITER WITH DUCHESS:
              service?

DUCHESS: Listen –

ELECTRICIAN AS WAITER:
              Can we be of any service, madam?

DUCHESS: Listen to me. I'd like a bottle of –

ELECTRICIAN AS WAITER:
              Certainly, madam.

DUCHESS: a bottle of claret and some sandwiches. Can you do
              that? I want some beef.

ELECTRICIAN AS WAITER:
              Now, madam.

DUCHESS: Bring me some wine. *(telephone down)* Bring me
              meat. Bring me wine. Fill me up. Anything you
              have. But come. Come in. Come in.

(After a time – door knock.)

DUCHESS: Come in.

(Door knock, louder, sinister.)

DUCHESS: *(long pause)*
>Come in.
>Yes, come in.

(Impressive entrance of Electrician as Waiter. As he comes forward into the room, it can be seen that behind him is the Hotel Manager, standing in the doorway. The doors are slowly closed over the next three or four lines.)

DUCHESS: What have you got there?

ELECTRICIAN AS WAITER:
>Claret, madam. And sandwiches, madam.

DUCHESS: What sandwiches?

ELECTRICIAN AS WAITER:
>Beef, madam.

DUCHESS: That will do very well. Wait one instant.

ELECTRICIAN AS WAITER:
>Yes, madam.

(He puts the tray down on the table. She goes over to the bed and sits down. She starts to rummage through her things which are lying in a pile on the bed, looking for money.)

DUCHESS: I may be some time. Sit down.

ELECTRICIAN AS WAITER:
>I am not permitted, madam.

(She stops and looks at him properly, as if for the first time.)

DUCHESS: You are permitted.

ELECTRICIAN AS WAITER:
>Yes madam.

DUCHESS: And you needn't call me madam every word. I
>don't require it.

ELECTRICIAN AS WAITER:
>Yes madam.

(He sits down heavily on a gilt wood chair behind him. She produces suddenly from her pile of clutter a big white note – not necessarily a realistic old five-pound note.)

DUCHESS: *(waving it at him)* Here. That will do.

ELECTRICIAN AS WAITER:
Will that do, madam?

DUCHESS: I said, that will do. Do you find it too much?

ELECTRICIAN AS WAITER:
They pay me here that much in a week.

DUCHESS: A week? *(she looks at the note – obviously more than she thought it was).* I see. You don't care to be given it as a present. You are unusual.

ELECTRICIAN AS WAITER:
No – *(stops himself from saying Madam)*

DUCHESS: Most men like presents. You are unusual. And a small present, too. You prefer not to be given things for nothing. You prefer to earn what you are given. Am I right?

ELECTRICIAN AS WAITER:
I would like to keep my job, madam.

DUCHESS: You will keep your job. I imagine you are a good waiter.

ELECTRICIAN AS WAITER: *(aggressive)*
Yes.

DUCHESS: Tell me, are you busy at the moment?

ELECTRICIAN AS WAITER:
Busy?

DUCHESS: The hotel seems full to me.

ELECTRICIAN AS WAITER:
The coronation.

DUCHESS: Oh, the coronation. I came here to escape that nonsense. Are you paid more when you are busy?

ELECTRICIAN AS WAITER:
No.

DUCHESS: How much are you paid?

ELECTRICIAN AS WAITER:
Paid?

DUCHESS: *N'importe.* Come here.

ELECTRICIAN AS WAITER:
I like my job, madam.

DUCHESS: Yes, I imagine you do. *On chuchote pas.*

ELECTRICIAN AS WAITER:
I'd like to keep my job, madam.

DUCHESS: They sack you for sitting down in a guest's room?

(Duchess puts on her lipstick, slowly, lewdly. Electrician as Waiter stands up, not nervously but – quite suddenly – sexily. He walks over to the bed where she is sitting and begins to walk around it.)

DUCHESS: There's no need for you to worry. It's quite safe.
You must have done this before. No need to worry –

ELECTRICIAN AS WAITER:
I never worry.

DUCHESS: We're undisturbed –

ELECTRICIAN AS WAITER:
Be quiet.

DUCHESS: No-one will come, the – my husband has no idea where I am. Yes, that will do. My husband has no idea. Forget who you are. Forget who I am. I have no idea. I do not know what I am doing. I have never done this before. I am deranged. I must be deranged. At these moments – yes, please – everything stops. Yes. Stop. I never asked you your name. You do not talk. I never ask. Be discreet, be good, be brutal. *(goes off into humming)*

ELECTRICIAN AS WAITER:
Be quiet.

(As the Electrician as Waiter has his orgasm a single flashbulb goes off. Awful noise of coughing from the Duchess, slowly subsiding.)

(Lights up.)

DUCHESS: That will do. Take the money.

ELECTRICIAN AS WAITER:
             How much?

DUCHESS: *(waving the note at him)*
             That much.

ELECTRICIAN AS WAITER:
             That much?

DUCHESS: Is it too much?

(Electrician as Waiter contemptuously takes it.)

ELECTRICIAN AS WAITER:
             Thank you, madam.

DUCHESS: Do you know who I am?

ELECTRICIAN AS WAITER:
             Oh yes, your Grace. Everyone knows who you are.
             All the boys, your Grace. Everyone. *On chuchote.*

DUCHESS: Have I seen you before?

ELECTRICIAN AS WAITER:
             Last April. The same story.

(He goes to the door before he goes back to the dresser and picks up the bottle of claret and the sandwiches. He exits with them to a new coughing fit of the Duchess.)

FIVE
Nineteen Fifty Three

(Maid as Mistress on the bed. Hotel Manager as Duke putting on a dressing gown over a dress shirt and black tie.)

MAID AS MISTRESS:
             Is Daddy squiffy?

HOTEL MANAGER AS DUKE:
             No.

MAID AS MISTRESS:
             Is Daddy squiffy?

HOTEL MANAGER AS DUKE:
> I don't think so.

MAID AS MISTRESS:
> Is Daddy bloody squiffy?

HOTEL MANAGER AS DUKE:
> Well – perhaps just a little.

MAID AS MISTRESS:
> Good Daddy. And where has he been to be so
> squiffy?

HOTEL MANAGER AS DUKE:
> The Hendersons. Good number. Grand style. You
> know, they said we'd never see that style again,
> after the war. And here we are and I can't
> remember such parties since my dancing days were
> over.

MAID AS MISTRESS:
> Queer, isn't it, darling? My father said quite the
> same thing my dear about the last war. And I can't
> remember it but by all accounts after the war was
> over –

HOTEL MANAGER AS DUKE: *(heavily)*
> I remember it. *(pause)*

MAID AS MISTRESS:
> And what has Daddy done with his baggage, then,
> the naughty naughty Daddy?

HOTEL MANAGER AS DUKE:
> Left her at the Hendersons holding court. There's
> some man she's sweet on.

MAID AS MISTRESS:
> Jel-jels?

HOTEL MANAGER AS DUKE:
> Not a bit, my dear. I know her through and
> through. I know she'd die rather than let a man
> touch her. But she likes her little pashes and her
> admirers and her boys.

MAID AS MISTRESS:

> I see. *(pause)* So is Daddy going to come to his girly, then?

HOTEL MANAGER AS DUKE:

> One moment.

(Takes off his dressing gown, sits on the bed and begins to take off his tie.)

> Give me some wine.

MAID AS MISTRESS:

> No glass, darling, or only a tooth glass.

HOTEL MANAGER AS DUKE:

> I've a trick worth two of that, my dear. Pass me the bottle.

(Passes him a bottle of champagne. He opens it and swigs from the bottle.)

HOTEL MANAGER AS DUKE:

> Darling?

MAID AS MISTRESS:

> I don't think so. I don't want to stink of it.

HOTEL MANAGER AS DUKE:

> Where does he think you are?

MAID AS MISTRESS:

> No idea. Why concern yourself?

HOTEL MANAGER AS DUKE:

> No concern, darling, just curiosity. Now turn over.

MAID AS MISTRESS: *(girlishly)*

> Why?

HOTEL MANAGER AS DUKE:

> Are you my little girl, my naughty naughty?

MAID AS MISTRESS: *(offhand)*

> If you want. *(sudden lechery)* You beast.

HOTEL MANAGER AS DUKE:

> You love it.

MAID AS MISTRESS:

> I love it. Where is she?

HOTEL MANAGER AS DUKE:
>Out. The Hendersons. *Ne t'inquiète pas.*

MAID AS MISTRESS:
>I thought she might be downstairs in the kitchen.

HOTEL MANAGER AS DUKE:
>Doubt if she knows where it is, to tell you the truth.

MAID AS MISTRESS:
>She knows quite well.

(pause)

HOTEL MANAGER AS DUKE:
>What do you mean?

MAID AS MISTRESS:
>Or so they say.

HOTEL MANAGER AS DUKE:
>What do you mean?

MAID AS MISTRESS:
>Nothing.

HOTEL MANAGER AS DUKE:
>I have to ask you what you mean by that.

MAID AS MISTRESS:
>Nothing. Is that a new footman?

HOTEL MANAGER AS DUKE:
>Which one? I have no idea. The Duchess looks after the staff.

MAID AS MISTRESS:
>So they say.

(He considers asking what she means but doesn't.)

MAID AS MISTRESS: *(stretching)*
>Is Daddy too squiffy for jumpies?

HOTEL MANAGER AS DUKE:
>Never too squiffy for you, my dear. Bottle, please.

MAID AS MISTRESS:
>You've had enough.

HOTEL MANAGER AS DUKE:
>
> Never enough. Never say no. Pass me the bottle.

(She does not. He reaches over and takes it.)

MAID AS MISTRESS:
>
> You shouldn't worry, you know.

HOTEL MANAGER AS DUKE:
>
> I don't.

MAID AS MISTRESS:
>
> About what people say.

HOTEL MANAGER AS DUKE:
>
> I don't care if people talk about us.

MAID AS MISTRESS:
>
> Not about us.

HOTEL MANAGER AS DUKE:
>
> What are you trying to say? *(pause)* Are you saying
> the Duchess is a whore?

MAID AS MISTRESS:
>
> No.

HOTEL MANAGER AS DUKE:
>
> Is she having an affair?

MAID AS MISTRESS:
>
> Not that I know of.

HOTEL MANAGER AS DUKE:
>
> Does she seduce my staff? Is that what you're telling
> me? The third footman and the temporary
> chauffeur? Is that what they say?

MAID AS MISTRESS:
>
> No. No. Don't you trust her? She's too good.
> She knows her place. She knows your trust.
> She would never do that. Never betray you.
> And for you, she would never question you.
> She adores you. She has no eyes for servants.
> Never in a thousand years, never in her life.
> Give her your faith, your every faith, give all you
> have.

It's completely false what people say.
Don't put any trust in foolish rumours.
Whatever they say. *(pause for his response)*
They like to talk. People always talk.
They always will. You know that. We all talk.
As for her, they'll talk until they've talked her out.
She's a topic, she's a conversation, she's a face in the
public prints.
> *They say her love is queer, perverted. Don't mind.*
> *For darling please remember you should be kind.*

You know that. And *on chuchote*. It may be nonsense.
It may be absurd. No-one may believe it. Don't
believe it.
You believe what the staff say?
Believe me. Believe her. Trust her. Don't doubt her.
Mais on chuchote.

HOTEL MANAGER AS DUKE:
For Christ's sake speak English.

(Pause)

MAID AS MISTRESS:
Very well. If you want to know the truth.
If you want to know what's going on.
There is her dresser, there is her case.
She doesn't lock them, she trusts you.
And inside there are her papers. Now look at them.

HOTEL MANAGER AS DUKE:
You've seen them?

MAID AS MISTRESS:
I've seen them. *(laughter)*

*(Hotel Manager as Duke gets up suddenly and Maid as Mistress stretches back.
He goes over to the trunk and starts pulling out clothes and letters. Papers scattered
everywhere, on the floor, on the bed, on the Maid as Mistress. He empties the
drawers of the dressing table – more papers – and, finally, in the last drawer, he
finds a camera. He rips it open and pulls out the film.)*

HOTEL MANAGER AS DUKE: *(end of song)*
That's it?

MAID AS MISTRESS:
> *That's it. She's in your clutches.*

(On the bed, they start to hunt through the papers. Curtain.)

INTERVAL

SIX
Nineteen Fifty Five

(Maid and Electrician as Rubberneckers outside the court.)

MAID AS RUBBERNECKER:
> Did she –

ELECTRICIAN AS RUBBERNECKER:
> Of course she did –

MAID AS RUBBERNECKER:
> And did he –

ELECTRICIAN AS RUBBERNECKER:
> Did he know? Of course he knew.

MAID AS RUBBERNECKER:
> He knew?

ELECTRICIAN AS RUBBERNECKER:
> He knew.

MAID AS RUBBERNECKER:
> Her own husband knowing, and never a word.

ELECTRICIAN AS RUBBERNECKER:
> Till now.

MAID AS RUBBERNECKER:
> Till now. I can't believe my own ears.

ELECTRICIAN AND MAID AS RUBBERNECKERS:
> They're not like us.

MAID AS RUBBERNECKER:
> From what I've heard I can't –

ELECTRICIAN AS RUBBERNECKER:
From what I've heard they've their own code.

MAID AS RUBBERNECKER:
A code?

ELECTRICIAN AS RUBBERNECKER:
It's all understood, and no-one minds.

MAID AS RUBBERNECKER:
A disgrace.

ELECTRICIAN AS RUBBERNECKER:
It's how they live.

MAID AS RUBBERNECKER:
Like monkeys –

ELECTRICIAN AS RUBBERNECKER:
Droit de Seigneur –

MAID AS RUBBERNECKER:
Droit de Seigneur?

ELECTRICIAN AS RUBBERNECKER:
Droit de Seigneur. She lived with all those men –

MAID AS RUBBERNECKER:
Do you mind?

ELECTRICIAN AS RUBBERNECKER:
Well, it's the truth and no more. And everyone
knew and nobody cared. And her husband took
photographs and his friends all saw them.

MAID AS RUBBERNECKER:
I can't believe it. No husband would.

ELECTRICIAN AS RUBBERNECKER:
It's the truth.

ELECTRICIAN AND MAID AS RUBBERNECKERS:
And she lived with men she hardly knew. She lived
with men she'd never met.

ELECTRICIAN AS RUBBERNECKER:
And he put up with it for years and years.

MAID AS RUBBERNECKER:
> And now he's spent her money.

ELECTRICIAN AND MAID AS RUBBERNECKERS:
> And there she is.

(Funeral Cortège. Rubberneckers retreat to the bed to bounce eagerly. Enter Duchess in an enormous black veil over a plain black daydress. She moves very slowly towards a chair, front left. Once she is settled, the Hotel Manager enters in a very grand pinstriped suit, no hat. He goes to the trunk and dresses in a judge's robe and wig.)

HOTEL MANAGER AS JUDGE:
> Order. Silence. Justice. Order. Silence. Madam.
> It is now my duty to pass judgment.
> And I shall proceed to do so.
> I imagine this court has witnessed many strange stories.
> Many episodes in private lives which had better not been made public.
> I myself have heard many horrors, and I have not shrunk from them.
> I have heard wonderful tales of men and beasts.
> Of murder and poison and reasonless lives.
> Queer acts after nightfall, and violence in silence.
> I have listened calmly to these tales, and I have listened to lies.
> I have listened to lies, and I have understood, without hatred, when I was lied to.
> I have lived long, and I have heard everything which a man may hear.
> Or so I had thought.
> This case began long months ago.
> It began as other cases do.
> It began without surprise, and with the usual sad anecdotes.
> I listened, and I made notes, and I considered the facts calmly.
> As the months went on, I was touched by these facts.
> The case affected me strangely.

I felt as if I were involved in it.

I felt as if I were assaulted by it.

For I have been here many years, and I expected to hear nothing new.

But now I have heard something new.

In this case, many of us have been transported to a world few of us were familiar with.

Many of us have not found it, on examination, an elevated one.

Many of us have not found the Duchess, on examination, an elevated person.

She is a woman who can be described as modern.

She is a woman who has no scruples, and the morals of a bed-post.

We have heard her sexual practices are those seldom found north of Marrakesh.

We have heard that she has an intimate knowledge of perversions which few of us can credit.

She is a woman unfit for marriage.

She is certainly a woman unfit to hold an ancient and honourable title.

She is a beast to an exceptional degree.

She is a Don Juan among women.

She is insatiable, unnatural and altogether fairly appalling.

I cannot continue.

I cannot express my horror at what I have discovered.

I find that the Duchess is entirely to blame for these sorry events.

I find that the Duke has no stain on his character.

I pity him for the mistake he has made, which frankly any of us might make.

I now proceed to costs.

(Duchess rises and comes to the front of the stage.)

Order. Justice. Silence. Order. Silence. Madam.

(She turns to the Hotel Manager as Judge. Exit Hotel Manager as Judge precipitously.)

MAID AS RUBBERNECKER:
Did you hear –

ELECTRICIAN AS RUBBERNECKER:
What he said?

MAID AS RUBBERNECKER:
Quite right.

ELECTRICIAN AS RUBBERNECKER:
Old trollop.

MAID AS RUBBERNECKER:
Do you mind?

ELECTRICIAN AS RUBBERNECKER:
It's him I feel sorry for –

MAID AS RUBBERNECKER:
I feel sorry for him.

ELECTRICIAN AND MAID AS RUBBERNECKERS:
Anyone might make the same mistake.
Anyone might marry by mistake.

ELECTRICIAN AS RUBBERNECKER:
Old trollop.

MAID AS RUBBERNECKER:
Old trollop. Is that her?

ELECTRICIAN AS RUBBERNECKER:
Is that her?

MAID AS RUBBERNECKER:
Is that her?

(Duchess slowly unveils herself.)

DUCHESS: So that is all.
                  I am judged.
                  I do not care.
                  And that was all.
                  There are worse things in life.
                  I am still loved.
                  I was loved before I was a Duchess, and I am a
                  Duchess still.

You. Summon my car.
I am still young.
I am still rich.
I can pay the costs.
I can face the consequences of my own actions, and
the consequences of lies told about me.
I do not care what lies are told about me, by
members of the middle classes.
That is what they are there for, the middle classes,
to lie.
I often wondered, and now I know.
And I am there to be beautiful.
I have a purpose in life, which is to be loved.
I know my purpose, and I know my place.
And I was brought up well, and I am a lady.
And I am a lady still, and I do not lie.
You. Now. Summon my car.
No. Today is no different from any other day, but
today.
Today I walk.

(Immensely grand tottery exit.)

MAID AND ELECTRICIAN AS RUBBERNECKERS:
    We've never been through –

*(Interrupted by small riot in the orchestra and a great electric storm of flashbulbs,
slowly becoming less frequent as the interlude progresses.)*

SEVEN
Nineteen Seventy

(Duchess, Maid as Society Journalist.)

*(The flashbulbs have continued intermittently throughout the last interlude. The
last flash is the flash of the women's magazine photographer (not present).)*

DUCHESS: I'd like to make one thing entirely clear. There are
certain matters I do not think I am prepared to talk
about.

MAID AS JOURNALIST:

> Yes, your Grace.

DUCHESS:

> I hope you understand what I mean. I hope you were told by my very good friend your editor that there are matters which I do not speak about, which nobody speaks about. I have nothing to say. Do I make myself clear?

MAID AS JOURNALIST:

> Yes, your Grace, but –

ELECTRICIAN AS DELIVERY BOY:

> *(entering with hat box)* Your Grace.

DUCHESS: Down there.

(He puts it down and exits.)

MAID AS JOURNALIST:

> Your Grace –

DUCHESS: Yes?

MAID AS JOURNALIST:

> You are known as a great survivor –

DUCHESS: *(displeased)* Oh really?

MAID AS JOURNALIST:

> You are known as a great reminder of a glorious society –

DUCHESS: *(still more displeased)* Oh really?

MAID AS JOURNALIST:

> You are beautiful now as you ever were.

DUCHESS: *(stonily pleased)* Yes I am.

MAID AS JOURNALIST:

> What are your secrets?

(Enter Electrician as Delivery Boy with another hat box.)

ELECTRICIAN AS DELIVERY BOY:

> Your Grace?

DUCHESS: Down there.

(He puts it down and leaves.)

MAID AS JOURNALIST:
        What are your secrets?

DUCHESS: My secrets?

MAID AS JOURNALIST:
        Your beauty secrets. The secret of your beauty.

DUCHESS: Ah yes. *(pause)*
        I wash in cold water seven times a day.

MAID AS JOURNALIST: *(writing)*
        Seven times.

DUCHESS: Never use hot. And never soap
        Hot water is drying to the skin. And soap is worse.

MAID AS JOURNALIST:
        Never hot.

DUCHESS: Never tire yourself.
        Never walk. I never walk. I never have.

MAID AS JOURNALIST:
        Never walk.

DUCHESS: Go to bed early and often.

MAID AS JOURNALIST:
        And often.

DUCHESS: Never allow things to affect you.
        Never let yourself worry.
        I never worry.

MAID AS JOURNALIST:
        Don't worry.

DUCHESS: And never touch money.
        I never touch money.
        I never carry money.
        I never deal with it.
        I have no need to.
        Cash is wearying and cash is soiling.

MAID AS JOURNALIST:
        What a beautiful room this is.

DUCHESS: I suppose it is.

MAID AS JOURNALIST: *(has stopped writing. Pause.)*
                       You are famous as a great hostess.
                       Perhaps the last of the great hostesses.

DUCHESS: The only one. There are none left.

(Electrician as Delivery Boy enters with a third hat-box. He goes to put it down.)

                       No, not that one. Bring it here.

(He brings it over. She opens it and produces an enormous little-girl Easter bonnet, piled high with chicks and daffodils and perhaps even a stuffed rabbit.)

                       Ah!

(She puts it on, ties a ribbon under her chin.)

                       None left. I am the only hostess left.
                       You see, I am the only one left who understands.
                       That will do, you may go.

(Waves a five-pound note at Electrician as Delivery Boy, who takes it and goes – slight suggestion of amazement at the hat.)

                       No-one entertains any more.
                       They sit and they look at their television screens.
                       They sit alone in their houses and never let anyone
                       in.
                       There are no parties any more. There are none.
                       There were such parties. And that has all gone.
                       Everything now is solitude, everyone is alone.
                       No-one visits, no-one comes.
                       Take this down, write it up.

MAID AS JOURNALIST:
                       Your Grace.

DUCHESS: There is no style. There is no elegance.

MAID AS JOURNALIST:
                       Style. Elegance.

DUCHESS: The great houses have gone.
                       There is rubble where there were palaces.
                       There are hotels where there were houses. Where

hostesses waited for their friends and their lovers
and their guests.
Hotels like this where the desperate live.
Take it down. There is no beauty.

MAID AS JOURNALIST:

Beauty.

DUCHESS:

Everywhere things are changing.
When one is driven in the street one never knows
what one will see.
One never sees a white face, not in the street, not
now.

MAID AS JOURNALIST:

Always wash in cold water.

DUCHESS:

Black men buy houses
Jews go everywhere
Concrete is everywhere
And buggery is legal.

MAID AS JOURNALIST:

Hot water is drying.

DUCHESS:

Never go out. It isn't safe.
Lock your door and stay inside.
There's only you, and slowly the terror subsides.
And outside there it's Africa.
The young fucking in the street –

MAID AS JOURNALIST:

Cold cream is best for the maturer skin.

DUCHESS:

The terror. The ugliness.
The shame they never had. The shame I never lost.
And now, what now, what then, outside?
Who comes? Who stays?
Who is there left to take me out?
My hatter? My wig maker? My priest?
What visitors come? Who stays?

(Electrician as Delivery Boy comes forward into the room with a letter on a silver
tray.)

ELECTRICIAN AS DELIVERY BOY:
                    Your grace.

DUCHESS: Here. Quickly.
                    (To Journalist, pointing) You. Knife.

(The Journalist hands her a paper knife. She tears the envelope open with it, places it between her teeth, and pulls out what is clearly an enormous bill.)

MAID AS JOURNALIST: *(gathering her things together)*
                    Thank you, your Grace.

(She and the Electrician back out of the room with increasing nervous speed.)

(Duchess has a paper knife between her teeth. As she mutters, she tears up the bill. By the end it is in a hundred tiny fragments lying around her.)

DUCHESS: Twenty three, forty seven, fifty eight, seventy nine, eighty one, eighty five, one hundred and four, one hundred and twelve, one hundred and sixteen, one hundred and thirty three, one hundred and fifty seven, one hundred and sixty eight, one hundred and eighty nine, one hundred and ninety one. . .

EIGHT
Nineteen Ninety

(The door opens as before, and the mysterious figure comes into the light. It is the Hotel Manager. Duchess is scrabbling on the floor for bits of paper and stuffing them into a trunk.)

DUCHESS: *(suddenly aware of the Hotel Manager)*
                    Who are you? How did you come in?

HOTEL MANAGER: Madam. I am the manager.

DUCHESS: The manager?

HOTEL MANAGER: You must have been expecting me.

DUCHESS: No, I have not been expecting you. I did not ask to see you.

HOTEL MANAGER: You must have read the letters we have sent you, madam.

DUCHESS: I have not.

HOTEL MANAGER: You have not.

DUCHESS: I have not.

HOTEL MANAGER: Very well, madam. I wonder if you are aware of the amount of money you owe the hotel.

DUCHESS: No, I am not.

HOTEL MANAGER: It is a good deal.

DUCHESS: You will be paid. It is not something I deal with.

HOTEL MANAGER: No payment has been received for eight months, madam.

DUCHESS: I will ask that you be paid directly.

HOTEL MANAGER: It is too late for that.
You have lived here too long.
It is time to vacate. You have lived here for a while.
The time to vacate always comes, and now it has come for you.
I have made inquiries. Your time is up.
You have nothing more. Everything is spent, madam,
Everything is used up. And now you must go.

DUCHESS: Not yet – I'm not – Not yet. I'm not quite ready. You must come back. You'll have to come back.
I haven't – I need to have my things packed.

HOTEL MANAGER: You see, it comes to everyone.
And everyone expects it. But you have not expected it.
And now it is here for you.

DUCHESS: I need more time.
A day, a week, a month. A month more. A week, a day.
Give me just one more day.

HOTEL MANAGER: Madam. Your car will have been ordered to be outside in one hour. *(He moves to the door)* Madam. Your Grace.

(He goes. Door closes behind him. Long pause.)

DUCHESS: *(facing away, motionless as if paralysed. Snaps out of it suddenly.)*
That will do. You may go.

(Distracts herself with some vehement activity.)

Servants used to know when to go.
They never stayed when they were not wanted.
(Pauses to reflect) I wonder how many servants I have
had in my life?
Probably too many to count. I had a nursemaid once
Who taught me how to walk straight, for whom
I brushed my hair a hundred times a night.
It shone. It was so hard to please her, and I tried so
hard,
And sometimes she was pleased, and I was pleased.
It made up for things. And later my maid,
My grown-up maid, who late at night
Would brush my hair and press my clothes
And told me off and was fond of me. And I was fond
of her.
She heard my secrets, and she kept them, too,
And really she was fond of me. She died, or so I
heard.
Restrictions
Legality
Commandments
There's nothing in all the world
Like...
There's nothing in all the world.
And there's no-one to dress me, and no-one to talk
to me.
And the only people who were ever good to me
were paid for it.

*(Motionless. Duchess goes very slowly to her trunk and pulls out a hand mirror
and a make-up bag. She begins to put on her lipstick in the mirror, but, half-way
through she stops, as if noticing something awful on her face. Suddenly throws
down mirror. Collects herself, and goes again to the trunk. Gets out a dressing case
and takes out a perfume bottle. She tries to pour some perfume out, but the bottle is*

empty. She throws it against the wall, where it breaks.)

DUCHESS: Broken. It's broken. Gone. It's the last thing I had.
                                And there is nothing left of me.
                                Nothing left beneath the sun.
                                Where are you nurse?
                                Where are you girl?
                                Gifts go and money goes.
                                I was young
                                I was rich
                                I was innocent

(Utter desperation, very emphatic – no song in orchestra.)

                                They wrote songs about me. Forgotten.

(Dreadful silence or dreadful noise but in any case no hint of the song. Door begins to open very slowly.)

                                Nurse, Nurse.
                                Come in. Please.

(Door opening – light very bright from without.)

                                Where are you all?
                                My servants. Loyal.
                                My friends. My friends.

(Hotel Manager enters.)

HOTEL MANAGER: Your car is here.

(Duchess slowly rouses herself.)

DUCHESS: I am not quite ready.

HOTEL MANAGER: Your car is here.

DUCHESS: Has nobody told you how to address me?

HOTEL MANAGER: Madam.

DUCHESS: There must be something I can do. There must be
                                something I can say.
                                Can I not persuade you to be patient?
                                Could you not have pity for me?
                                Come and talk to me.

Come and sit by me.
Hold me, please.
It's so long since I've been held.
People used to like to hold me.
Spare me one moment, and come here for me. Just
for me.
Dear boy, just one second. It won't take long, and
I'll make you happy.
Could you not be fond of me?
A little more fond? A little patient?
Be kind to me.
Be kind.

(She makes a blatant assault on him.)

HOTEL MANAGER: Your car is here. That is all, madam.

(He drags the trunk to the door and exits. Complete breakdown of Duchess lying on bed. After some time she raises herself and goes to the gramophone. She looks round in a desultory way for the record, can't find it, puts the needle on the turntable. Hideous white noise of needle going round the rubber turntable. Exit clutching gramophone. GHOST EPILOGUE. The stage begins to darken into dusk. After a time the Electrician and the Maid emerge surprisingly from underneath the bed. They begin to strip the bed (sheet-folding Tango – statuesque poses). Electrician reaches across the bed and gropes the Maid. She jumps out of reach. He jumps onto the bed and she jumps on top of him. She slaps him playfully. He slaps her back.)

MAID: *(stern)*   Enough.

ELECTRICIAN: *(lewd)* Or too much!

(The electrician attempts to roll onto the Maid; the Maid makes a surprising exit as the curtain falls.)

End